made this book

T FOR YOU

because...

(a really good reason)

P.S.

(one more nice thing)

color in the pictures

MOM, when I'm your age, I hope I'm as...

fancy as you

honest as you

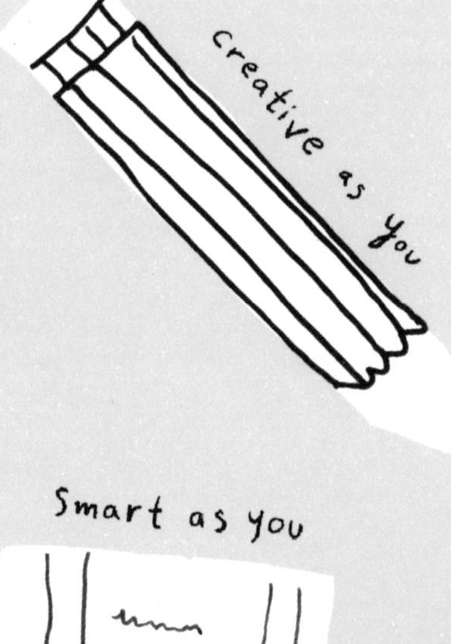

creative as you

grown-up as you

smart as you

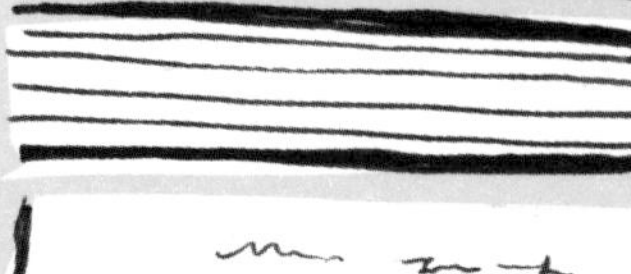

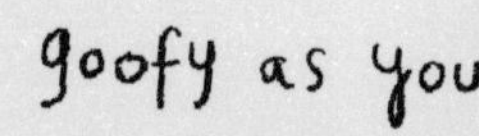

goofy as you

funny as you

caring as you

generous as you

strong as you

happy as you

brave as you

If There Was a
SUPER
MOM
CONTEST,
you'd win
AWARDS for:

BEST

MOST EXCELLENT
GREATEST

When I'm sick, you always...

____

____.

(nice thing she does for me)

When I'm Grumpy, you...

____

____.

(how she makes me smile)

You make
the BEST DAYS
EVEN BETTER when you...
(amazing thing she does for me)

I wouldn't trade
YOU for...

✓ check a box (or two!) ✓

- [ ] a trillion dollars
- [ ] a house made of marshmallows
- [ ] five jumbo jets
- [ ] every ice cream sandwich on Earth
- [ ] a circus of fluffy cats
- [ ] actual superpowers

BECAUSE _

(a very good reason)

IF WE HAD OUR OWN PLANET,
IT WOULD BE CALLED:

IT WOULD HAVE:

(choose one word from each creature)

floating
robot
moving
waterslide
underwater
laser
candy
giant

playgrounds
cities
highways
forests
domes
butlers
sidewalks
unicorns

AND we'd _________________________ every day.

(fun thing we'd do together)

ONE DAY,

I hope we go to .... ,
(faraway Place)

and eat .... ,
(favorite treat)

AND take lots of pictures like this one:

✓ check your favorite boxes ✓

- [ ] train a shark to catch fish
- [ ] make our own city
- [ ] make sandcastles all day
- [ ] build a raft and become pirates
- [ ] go wild, like monkeys
- [ ] ride turtles all the way home
- [ ] ______________________

(create your own)

This is what our island would look like!

Because, **MOM**, you're

....,

(why she's special)

And **I LOVE YOU** more than

....

(something I love a lot)

When I'm with you, I'm sooooooo

....

(how she makes me feel)

LOVE,...................................

P.S. Here's one more drawing of us,
having the MOST FUN EVER!